ITALY TRAVEL GUIDE

GUIDE

"Exploring Italy: A Journey Through History, Culture, and Cuisine"

THOMAS MOORE

TABLE OF CONTENT

Introduction to Italy

Italy, a land of timeless beauty and rich cultural heritage, beckons travellers with its irresistible charm and allure. Nestled in the heart of the Mediterranean, this enchanting country boasts a tapestry of landscapes, from the sun-kissed shores of the Amalfi Coast to the majestic peaks of the Alps. Steeped in history, Italy is a living museum, where ancient ruins, Renaissance masterpieces, and mediaeval villages coexist harmoniously with modern life.

From the iconic landmarks of Rome to the romantic canals of Venice, Italy's cities are vibrant hubs of art, architecture, and gastronomy. Each region offers a unique sensory experience, from the aromatic flavours of Tuscany to the fiery spirit of Naples. But beyond its bustling metropolises lie hidden treasures waiting to be discovered – secluded beaches, picturesque vineyards, and hilltop towns frozen in time.

Italy is more than just a destination; it's a journey through time, where every cobblestone street and crumbling ruin tells a story. Whether you're indulging in a leisurely passeggiata or savouring a gelato by the Trevi Fountain, Italy captivates the soul and leaves an indelible mark on all who wander its storied paths. So, come along on an adventure of a lifetime and immerse yourself in the magic of Italy. La dolce vita awaits.

Chapter 1

Planning Your Trip

Before embarking on your Italian adventure, it's essential to make thorough preparations to ensure a smooth and enjoyable journey. Here are some key aspects to consider:

Timing: Decide when to visit Italy based on your preferences and interests. Each season offers its unique charm, whether it's the vibrant colours of spring, the balmy summer days, the crisp autumn air, or the festive atmosphere of winter.

Visa Requirements: Check the visa requirements for your nationality well in advance. Ensure your passport is valid for at least six months beyond your intended stay in Italy.

Packing Essentials: Pack according to the season and activities planned. Comfortable walking shoes, lightweight clothing, a travel adapter, and a versatile daypack are essential items. Don't forget to include any specific items you may need for activities such as hiking or beach outings.

Accommodation: Research and book accommodation that suits your budget and preferences. Options range from luxury hotels and boutique B&Bs to budget-friendly hostels and vacation rentals. Consider factors such as location, amenities, and reviews from previous guests.

Transportation: Plan how you'll get around Italy, whether by train, bus, car rental, or domestic flights. Italy's extensive public transportation network makes it easy to navigate between cities and regions. Booking tickets in advance can often save time and money, especially for popular routes.

Travel Insurance: Consider purchasing travel insurance to protect yourself against unforeseen circumstances such as trip cancellations, medical emergencies, or lost luggage.

Currency and Budgeting: Familiarise yourself with the local currency (Euro) and plan your budget accordingly. Italy offers a range of dining options, from budget-friendly trattorias to Michelin-starred restaurants, so budget accordingly for meals and activities.

Language and Cultural Etiquette: While English is widely spoken in tourist areas, learning some basic Italian phrases can enhance your experience and interactions with locals. Familiarise yourself with Italian customs and cultural norms to show respect and avoid unintentional faux pas.

By carefully planning each aspect of your trip, you'll be well-prepared to make the most of your time in Italy and create unforgettable memories that will last a lifetime. Buon viaggio!

When to Go

Deciding when to visit Italy depends on your preferences and what experiences you seek. Here's a breakdown by season:

Spring (March to May): Spring brings mild temperatures and blooming landscapes, making it an ideal time for sightseeing and outdoor activities. Crowds are thinner compared to summer, and you'll enjoy pleasant weather for exploring cities, hiking in the countryside, and visiting gardens.

Summer (June to August): Summer is peak tourist season in Italy, with long days of sunshine and warm temperatures, especially in the south. It's perfect for beach vacations along the Amalfi Coast or Sicily and for enjoying outdoor festivals and events. However, popular destinations can be crowded, and prices tend to be higher.

Autumn (September to November): Autumn offers comfortable temperatures, fewer crowds, and picturesque landscapes as vineyards turn golden and trees display their fall colours. It's an excellent time for food and wine festivals, truffle hunting, and exploring historic sites without the summer crowds.

Winter (December to February): Winter in Italy varies by region, with milder temperatures in the south and colder weather in the north and mountains. Ski resorts in the Alps and Dolomites are popular destinations for winter sports enthusiasts. Cities like Rome, Florence, and Venice are less crowded, and you can experience festive events such as Christmas markets and carnival celebrations.

Ultimately, the best time to visit Italy depends on your preferences for weather, crowds, and activities. Consider what experiences are most important to you and plan accordingly. Keep in mind that booking accommodations and transportation in advance, especially during peak seasons, can help ensure a smooth and enjoyable trip.

Visa Requirements

Schengen Visa: If you're a citizen of a country that's not part of the European Union or the Schengen Area, you may need a Schengen Visa to visit Italy for tourism, business, or family visits. The Schengen Visa allows you to travel within the Schengen Area, which includes Italy, without needing additional visas for each country.

Exemptions: Some countries have visa exemptions, allowing their citizens to visit Italy and other Schengen countries for short stays (usually up to 90 days within 180 days) without a visa. These exemptions often apply to citizens of the United States, Canada, Australia, and many other countries. However, the specific requirements and duration of stay allowed without a visa may vary.

Long-Term Visas: If you plan to stay in Italy for longer than 90 days or for purposes such as work, study, or family reunification, you may need to apply for a long-term visa or residence permit before your arrival. Requirements and application procedures for long-term visas vary depending on the purpose of your stay and your nationality.

Application Process: To apply for a Schengen Visa or a long-term visa, you'll typically need to submit an application form, passport photos, a valid passport, travel itinerary, proof of accommodation, proof of sufficient funds to cover your expenses, travel insurance, and any additional documents required by the Italian consulate or embassy in your country.

Processing Time: Visa processing times can vary depending on the embassy or consulate and the time of year. It's advisable to apply for your visa well in advance of your planned travel dates to allow for processing and any additional requirements.

Consultation: For specific information about visa requirements and application procedures based on your nationality and travel plans, it's best to consult the website of the Italian embassy or consulate in your country or seek guidance from a qualified immigration advisor.

Remember to check the most up-to-date visa requirements and regulations before planning your trip to Italy, as they may change over time.

Packing Essentials

Travel Documents: Passport, visa (if required), travel insurance, itinerary, hotel reservations, and any other important documents in a secure travel wallet or pouch.

Clothing: Pack lightweight, breathable clothing suitable for the season and activities planned. Include comfortable walking shoes, sandals, or sneakers for exploring cities and cobblestone streets. If visiting churches or religious sites, bring clothing that covers shoulders and knees.

Weather Gear: Check the weather forecast for your destination and pack accordingly. Bring a lightweight jacket or sweater for cooler evenings, a rain jacket or umbrella for rainy days, and a hat and sunglasses for sun protection.

Electronics: Don't forget your smartphone, charger, camera, and any other electronic devices you'll need. Consider bringing a portable power bank for charging on the go.

Adapters and Converters: Italy uses the Europlug (Type C) electrical outlet, so bring a universal adapter if your devices have different plug types. If your devices require a different voltage, also pack a voltage converter.

Medications: Bring any prescription medications you'll need for the duration of your trip, along with over-the-counter medications for common ailments such as headaches, allergies, and motion sickness.

Toiletries: Pack travel-sized toiletries such as shampoo, conditioner, body wash, toothpaste, and sunscreen. Remember to adhere to TSA regulations for liquids and gels if flying.

Travel Accessories: Consider bringing a lightweight daypack for sightseeing, a reusable water bottle, a travel guidebook or map, a compact travel umbrella, and a money belt or pouch for carrying valuables.

Travel Health Kit: Include items such as hand sanitizer, disinfectant wipes, bandages, insect repellent, and any personal hygiene products you prefer.

Entertainment: Bring books, magazines, or e-readers for downtime during travel or relaxing moments. Don't forget headphones or earbuds for listening to music or podcasts.

Remember to pack light and leave room for souvenirs or gifts you may purchase during your trip. It's also a good idea to make copies of important documents and keep them in a separate location from the originals. With these essentials packed, you'll be well-prepared for a memorable and enjoyable journey to Italy!

Chapter 2

Regions of Italy

Italy is divided into several distinct regions, each offering its own unique culture, cuisine, and landscapes. Here are some of the main regions of Italy:

Northern Italy:

Lombardy: Home to fashion capital Milan, Lake Como, and the picturesque cities of Bergamo and Mantua.

Veneto: Famous for romantic Venice, historic Verona, and the Prosecco wine region.

Piedmont: Known for its exquisite cuisine, including truffles and Barolo wine, as well as the city of Turin.

Emilia-Romagna: Renowned for its culinary delights such as Bologna's pasta, Parma's ham, and Modena's balsamic vinegar.

Trentino-Alto Adige: Offers stunning Alpine scenery, including the Dolomites mountain range and the charming town of Bolzano.

Central Italy:

Tuscany: Famous for its rolling hills, vineyards, and Renaissance art cities such as Florence, Siena, and Pisa.

Umbria: Known as the "**Green Heart of Italy**" for its lush landscapes and mediaeval hilltop towns like Assisi and Perugia.

Lazio: Home to the Eternal City of Rome, with its ancient ruins, Vatican City, and coastal towns like Ostia and Anzio.

Southern Italy:

Campania: Features the vibrant city of Naples, the archaeological sites of Pompeii and Herculaneum, and the stunning Amalfi Coast.

Apulia (Puglia): Known for its whitewashed trulli houses in Alberobello, picturesque coastline, and unique cuisine.

Calabria: Offers rugged coastline, pristine beaches, and traditional villages nestled in the mountains.

Basilicata: Known for the ancient city of Matera, with its cave dwellings and historic sassi districts.

Islands:

Sicily: Italy's largest island, boasting ancient Greek temples, and Baroque architecture in cities like Palermo, and Mount Etna, Europe's most active volcano.

Sardinia: Known for its stunning beaches, rugged interior landscape, and prehistoric archaeological sites such as the nuraghe.

Each region of Italy has its distinct character and attractions, offering visitors a diverse range of experiences to enjoy. Whether you're exploring the art and history of Florence, indulging in the culinary delights of Emilia-Romagna, or soaking up the sun on the Amalfi Coast, there's something for everyone to discover in Italy's rich tapestry of regions.

Chapter 3

Top Destinations

Italy is brimming with iconic destinations that showcase its rich history, culture, and natural beauty. Here are some of the top destinations you won't want to miss:

Rome: The Eternal City is a treasure trove of ancient wonders, including the Colosseum, Roman Forum, and Pantheon. Explore Vatican City to see St. Peter's Basilica and the Sistine Chapel, and toss a coin into the Trevi Fountain for good luck.

Florence: Birthplace of the Renaissance, Florence is home to world-renowned art and architecture. Marvel at Michelangelo's David in the Accademia Gallery, admire the Duomo's impressive dome and stroll across the iconic Ponte Vecchio bridge.

Venice: Explore the enchanting canals of Venice by gondola or Vaporetto, visit St. Mark's Basilica and the Doge's Palace in Piazza San Marco, and get lost in the maze-like streets of the historic centre.

Milan: Italy's fashion and design capital offers a blend of historic and modern attractions. Admire Leonardo da Vinci's masterpiece, The Last Supper, in the Santa Maria delle Grazie church, shop in the upscale boutiques of the Quadrilatero della Moda, and visit the iconic Milan Cathedral.

Naples: Immerse yourself in the lively atmosphere of Naples, where you can sample authentic Neapolitan pizza, explore the archaeological treasures of the Naples National Archaeological Museum, and take a day trip to the ancient ruins of Pompeii and Herculaneum.

These are just a few highlights of Italy's top destinations, each offering its unique charm and attractions. Whether you're drawn to the ancient history of Rome, the art of Florence, the romance of Venice, the fashion of Milan, or the vibrant culture of Naples, you're sure to be captivated by Italy's timeless allure.

Rome

Rome, the Eternal City, is a captivating blend of ancient history, Renaissance art, and vibrant modern life. Here's what makes Rome such a compelling destination:

Ancient Ruins: Explore iconic landmarks such as the Colosseum, where gladiators once battled, and the Roman Forum, the heart of ancient Rome's political and social life. Don't miss the majestic Pantheon, a marvel of ancient engineering with its domed roof and Oculus.

Vatican City: Visit the world's smallest independent state, home to St. Peter's Basilica, one of the largest churches in the world, and the Vatican Museums, housing priceless artworks including Michelangelo's Sistine Chapel ceiling.

Historic Squares: Wander through Rome's picturesque squares, such as Piazza Navona, adorned with elegant fountains and Baroque architecture, and Piazza di Spagna, where you'll find the Spanish Steps and Bernini's Fountain of the Barcaccia.

Fountains and Landmarks: Toss a coin into the Trevi Fountain to ensure your return to Rome, marvel at the grandeur of the Altare della Patria (Victor Emmanuel II Monument), and climb the Spanish Steps for panoramic views of the city.

Culinary Delights: Indulge in Rome's culinary delights, from classic pasta dishes like carbonara and cacao e pepe to authentic Roman-style pizza. Be sure to sample traditional Roman street food such as supplì (fried rice balls) and gelato from artisanal gelaterias.

Art and Museums: Discover masterpieces of art and sculpture in Rome's museums, including the Galleria Borghese with works by Bernini and Caravaggio, and the Capitoline Museums, home to ancient Roman artefacts and sculptures.

Charming Neighbourhoods: Get lost in Rome's charming neighbourhoods, from the historic streets of Trastevere lined with cobblestone alleys and lively trattorias to the trendy boutiques and cafes of Monti.

Rome's timeless beauty, rich history, and vibrant culture make it a must-visit destination for travellers seeking to immerse themselves in the wonders of the Eternal City.

Florence

Florence, the birthplace of the Renaissance, is a city steeped in art, history, and culture. Here's why Florence is one of Italy's top destinations:

Artistic Masterpieces: Marvel at world-renowned artworks by masters such as Michelangelo, Leonardo da Vinci, and Botticelli. Visit the Uffizi Gallery to see iconic paintings like Botticelli's "The Birth of Venus" and Leonardo's "Annunciation."

Architectural Wonders: Admire Florence's stunning architecture, including the magnificent Florence Cathedral (Duomo) with its iconic dome by Brunelleschi, Giotto's Bell Tower, and the Baptistery's golden doors.

Renaissance Landmarks: Explore the historic heart of Florence at Piazza della Signoria, home to the Palazzo Vecchio and the outdoor sculpture gallery of Loggia dei Lanzi. Nearby, visit the Ponte Vecchio, Florence's oldest bridge lined with jewellery shops.

Cultural Institutions: Immerse yourself in Florence's rich cultural heritage at institutions such as the Accademia Gallery, where you can see Michelangelo's famous sculpture "David," and the Bargello Museum, housing Renaissance sculptures and decorative arts.

Mediaeval Streets: Wander through Florence's charming mediaeval streets and discover hidden gems such as the Basilica of Santa Croce, the final resting place of Michelangelo, Galileo, and

Machiavelli, and the Oltrarno district, known for its artisan workshops and authentic trattorias.

Gardens and Parks: Escape the hustle and bustle of the city in Florence's tranquil green spaces, including the Boboli Gardens, a sprawling Renaissance garden with panoramic views of the city, and the romantic Bardini Gardens overlooking the Arno River.

Culinary Delights: Indulge in Tuscan cuisine at Florence's traditional trattorias and gourmet restaurants. Sample local specialties such as ribollita (Tuscan bean soup), bistecca alla Fiorentina (Florentine steak), and gelato from artisanal gelaterias.

Cultural Events: Experience Florence's vibrant cultural scene with events such as the Maggio Musicale Fiorentino, one of Italy's oldest music festivals, and the Florence Biennale, showcasing contemporary art from around the world.

With its timeless beauty, artistic treasures, and romantic ambiance, Florence is a destination that captures the hearts of visitors from around the globe.

Venice

Venice, the *"City of Canals,"* is a captivating destination renowned for its romantic ambiance, stunning architecture, and unique waterways. Here's what makes Venice one of Italy's top destinations:

Grand Canal: Experience the enchanting beauty of Venice by taking a leisurely ride along the Grand Canal on a traditional gondola or vaporetto (water bus). Admire the elegant palaces, historic bridges, and bustling activity along this iconic waterway.

St. Mark's Square: Discover the heart of Venice at Piazza San Marco (St. Mark's Square), home to St. Mark's Basilica with its dazzling mosaics, the imposing Campanile (bell tower), and the historic Doge's Palace, once the seat of Venetian power.

Venetian Architecture: Wander through Venice's labyrinthine streets and admire its architectural treasures, including the Gothic-style Doge's Palace, the Renaissance masterpiece of the Church of Santa Maria dei Frari, and the Byzantine-inspired St. Mark's Basilica.

Venetian Islands: Explore the enchanting islands of the Venetian Lagoon, such as Murano, famous for its centuries-old tradition of glassmaking, and Burano, known for its colourful houses and exquisite lacework.

Cultural Institutions: Immerse yourself in Venice's rich cultural heritage at museums such as the Gallerie dell'Accademia, showcasing Venetian art from the Middle Ages to the Renaissance, and the Peggy Guggenheim Collection, featuring modern and contemporary art.

Venetian Cuisine: Indulge in Venetian cuisine at traditional bacari (wine bars) and trattorias, where you can sample local specialties such as Cicchetti (Venetian tapas), risotto al nero di sepia (risotto with cuttlefish ink), and sarde in saor (marinated sardines).

Venetian Festivals: Experience the magic of Venice's festivals, including the world-famous Carnival with its elaborate masks and costumes, and the historic Regata Storica, a colorful procession of gondolas and rowing boats along the Grand Canal.

Artisan Workshops: Discover Venice's artisanal traditions by visiting workshops where craftsmen create exquisite glassware, handmade masks, and intricate lacework, keeping centuries-old techniques alive.

With its timeless beauty, rich history, and romantic allure, Venice offers a truly unforgettable experience for visitors seeking to immerse themselves in the magic of this unique city on the water.

Milan

Milan, Italy's fashion and design capital, is a dynamic metropolis known for its cosmopolitan atmosphere, historic landmarks, and vibrant cultural scene. Here's what makes Milan one of Italy's top destinations:

Fashion and Shopping: Explore Milan's world-famous fashion district, Quadrilatero della Moda, home to high-end boutiques, luxury brands, and designer flagship stores. Don't miss the chance to shop for Italian fashion and accessories along Via Montenapoleone, Via della Spiga, and Via Manzoni.

Milan Cathedral (Duomo): Admire the breathtaking Gothic architecture of Milan's iconic cathedral, the Duomo di Milano. Climb to the rooftop terrace for panoramic views of the city and marvel at the intricate details of the cathedral's marble façade and spires.

Leonardo da Vinci's Last Supper: Experience one of the world's most famous artworks at the Convent of Santa Maria delle Grazie. Book tickets in advance to see Leonardo da Vinci's masterpiece, "The Last Supper," which depicts the biblical scene of Jesus and his disciples.

La Scala Opera House: Attend a performance at Teatro alla Scala, one of the most prestigious opera houses in the world. Experience the magic of opera, ballet, or classical music in this historic venue, which has hosted legendary artists such as Maria Callas and Giuseppe Verdi.

Sforza Castle: Explore the imposing Sforza Castle, a mediaeval fortress and former residence of the ruling Visconti and Sforza families. Today, the castle houses several museums and art collections, including Michelangelo's unfinished sculpture, the "***Rondanini Pietà***."

Brera District: Wander through the picturesque streets of the Brera neighbourhood, known for its charming cafes, art galleries, and historic buildings. Visit the Pinacoteca di Brera, an art museum housing masterpieces by Italian and European artists.

Navigli Canals: Discover Milan's vibrant nightlife scene along the Navigli, a network of picturesque canals lined with bars, restaurants, and live music venues. Enjoy an evening stroll along the canal banks or hop on a boat cruise to explore the waterways.

Contemporary Architecture: Marvel at Milan's modern skyline, dotted with architectural landmarks such as the futuristic Piazza Gae Aulenti, the sleek skyscrapers of Porta Nuova, and the innovative Fondazione Prada arts complex designed by architect Rem Koolhaas.

With its blend of historical grandeur, cutting-edge design, and cultural richness, Milan offers a dynamic and eclectic experience for travellers seeking to explore Italy's fashion capital.

Naples

Naples, the vibrant capital of Italy's Campania region, is a city bursting with energy, history, and culinary delights. Here's what makes Naples one of Italy's top destinations:

Pizza: Naples is the birthplace of pizza, and no visit is complete without indulging in a traditional Neapolitan pizza. Head to one of the city's historic pizzerias, such as Da Michele or Sorbillo, to savour the authentic flavours of Margherita or Marinara pizza.

Historic Centre: Explore the historic heart of Naples, a UNESCO World Heritage Site, where narrow streets are lined with colourful buildings, bustling markets, and hidden chapels. Don't miss the Spaccanapoli street, which divides the city into two halves, and the lively atmosphere of Piazza Bellini.

Archaeological Sites: Discover Naples' ancient past at sites such as Pompeii and Herculaneum, which were buried by the eruption of

Mount Vesuvius in 79 AD. Explore the remarkably preserved ruins of these Roman towns, including villas, temples, and amphitheatres.

National Archaeological Museum: Delve into Naples' rich history at the National Archaeological Museum, home to an extensive collection of artefacts from Pompeii, Herculaneum, and other archaeological sites. Highlights include mosaics, frescoes, and the Farnese Bull sculpture.

Castel dell'Ovo: Visit the Castel dell'Ovo, a mediaeval castle perched on a peninsula overlooking the Bay of Naples. Explore the castle's courtyards and enjoy panoramic views of the city and Mount Vesuvius from its ramparts.

Waterfront Promenade: Take a stroll along the Lungomare, Naples' scenic waterfront promenade, which offers stunning views of the bay and the imposing Castel dell'Ovo. Relax in one of the seaside cafes or enjoy a sunset walk along the seafront.

Street Food and Markets: Experience Naples' culinary scene at its vibrant street markets, such as the Mercato di Porta Nolana and the Mercato di Pignasecca. Sample local specialties like frittelle (fried dough balls) and sfogliatella (ricotta-filled pastries).

Cultural Events: Immerse yourself in Naples' cultural heritage at events such as the Festival of San Gennaro, celebrating the city's patron saint, and the Maggio dei Monumenti, when historic sites and monuments open their doors to the public.

With its lively street life, rich history, and mouthwatering cuisine, Naples offers a sensory feast for travellers seeking an authentic Italian experience.

Chapter 4

Hidden Gems

Discovering hidden gems is one of the joys of travelling, and Italy is full of them. Here are some lesser-known treasures worth exploring:

Procida: Escape the crowds of Capri and Ischia and visit the charming island of Procida in the Bay of Naples. With its pastel-coloured houses, secluded beaches, and tranquil atmosphere, Procida is a hidden gem waiting to be discovered.

Ravenna Mosaics: Explore the stunning Byzantine mosaics of Ravenna, a UNESCO World Heritage Site. Admire the intricate designs and vibrant colours of these ancient artworks in churches and monuments such as the Basilica of San Vitale and the Mausoleum of Galla Placidia.

Matera: Step back in time in the ancient city of Matera, known for its unique cave dwellings and historic sassi districts. Explore the labyrinthine streets, visit the rock-hewn churches, and marvel at the breathtaking views of the Sassi di Matera from across the ravine.

Orvieto Underground: Descend into the hidden world beneath the mediaeval hilltop town of Orvieto to explore its underground tunnels, wells, and caves. Learn about the city's fascinating history and engineering feats on a guided tour of these subterranean passageways.

Villa d'Este: Escape the crowds of Rome and visit the Renaissance gardens of Villa d'Este in Tivoli. Explore the terraced gardens, fountains, and water features of this UNESCO World Heritage Site, which offers a peaceful retreat from the city.

Cinque Terre Villages: Discover the lesser-known villages of Cinque Terre, such as Corniglia and Manarola, away from the tourist crowds. Hike along scenic trails, swim in hidden coves, and savour fresh seafood in local trattorias overlooking the Mediterranean Sea.

Villa Romana del Casale: Journey to the heart of Sicily to explore the Roman villa of Villa Romana del Casale, famous for its well-preserved mosaics depicting scenes of daily life and ancient mythology. Marvel at the intricate designs and vibrant colours of these ancient artworks.

Valley of the Temples: Explore the ancient Greek ruins of the Valley of the Temples in Agrigento, Sicily. Wander among the well-preserved Doric temples, including the Temple of Concordia, and soak up the atmosphere of this archaeological wonder overlooking the Mediterranean Sea.

These hidden gems offer a glimpse into Italy's rich history, culture, and natural beauty, away from the tourist crowds. Whether you're exploring ancient ruins, wandering through mediaeval towns, or enjoying the tranquillity of secluded islands, you're sure to be enchanted by Italy's lesser-known treasures.

Off-the-Beaten-Path Towns

Exploring off-the-beaten-path towns in Italy is a rewarding way to discover hidden gems and experience the authentic charm of the country. Here are some lesser-known towns worth visiting:

Matera, Basilicata: Matera is famous for its ancient cave dwellings, known as "Sassi," which have been inhabited for thousands of years. Explore the narrow alleyways, cave churches, and rock-cut architecture of this UNESCO World Heritage Site.

Mantua (Mantova), Lombardy: Tucked away in the Lombardy region, Mantua is a Renaissance gem with a rich artistic and cultural heritage. Visit the Palazzo Ducale, the Rotonda di San Lorenzo, and the stunning frescoes of the Palazzo Te.

Spello, Umbria: Located in the heart of Umbria, Spello is a picturesque hilltop town known for its flower-lined streets, mediaeval architecture, and panoramic views of the surrounding countryside. Don't miss the chance to explore the town's historic churches and charming piazzas.

Montepulciano, Tuscany: Situated in the scenic countryside of Tuscany, Montepulciano is renowned for its mediaeval hilltop setting, Renaissance palaces, and world-class wine. Wander through the cobblestone streets, sample the famous Vino Nobile di Montepulciano, and enjoy panoramic views from the town's fortified walls.

Alberobello, Apulia (Puglia): Alberobello is famous for its unique trulli houses, and traditional dry-stone dwellings with conical roofs. Explore the picturesque streets lined with trulli, visit the Trullo Sovrano, and learn about the history and craftsmanship of these iconic structures.

Civita di Bagnoregio, Lazio: Civita di Bagnoregio is a mediaeval hill town perched atop a tufa rock plateau in the Lazio region. Accessible only by a pedestrian bridge, Civita di Bagnoregio feels like a step back in time with its ancient architecture and breathtaking views of the surrounding countryside.

Cefalù, Sicily: Nestled along the northern coast of Sicily, Cefalù is a charming seaside town known for its sandy beaches, mediaeval streets, and Norman cathedral. Stroll along the waterfront promenade, explore the winding alleyways of the historic centre, and hike up to the ancient Rocca di Cefalù for panoramic views of the town and sea.

San Gimignano, Tuscany: Often overshadowed by larger Tuscan cities, San Gimignano is a hidden gem known for its mediaeval towers, well-preserved historic centre, and scenic countryside. Climb the Torre Grossa for panoramic views, sample local Vernaccia wine, and wander through the town's artisan workshops and galleries.

These off-the-beaten-path towns offer a glimpse into Italy's diverse landscapes, rich history, and unique cultural heritage. Whether you're exploring ancient cave dwellings, mediaeval hilltop villages, or seaside towns, you're sure to discover unforgettable experiences and hidden treasures along the way.

Secret Beaches

Exploring secret beaches is a delightful way to uncover hidden gems and enjoy the beauty of Italy's coastline. Here are some lesser-known beaches worth discovering:

Cala Goloritzé, Sardinia: Tucked away along the Gulf of Orosei, Cala Goloritzé is a secluded cove with crystal-clear turquoise waters and a stunning natural limestone arch. Accessible only by boat or a challenging hike, this pristine beach is a paradise for snorkelers and nature lovers.

Cala Mariolu, Sardinia: Another hidden gem on the Gulf of Orosei, Cala Mariolu is known for its dramatic cliffs, white pebble beach, and vibrant marine life. Accessible by boat or hiking trail, this secluded cove offers excellent snorkelling and swimming opportunities.

Cala Pulcino, Sicily: Located on the island of Lampedusa, Cala Pulcino is a remote beach known for its powdery white sand, turquoise waters, and rugged cliffs. Accessible only by boat or a challenging hike, this pristine cove is a sanctuary for sea turtles and marine life.

Spiaggia di Tuerredda, Sardinia: Situated on the southern coast of Sardinia, Spiaggia di Tuerredda is a hidden gem with golden sand, clear waters, and stunning views of the nearby Isola di Tuerredda. Despite its beauty, this beach remains relatively uncrowded, making it the perfect spot for relaxation and swimming.

Marina di Pisciotta, Campania: Nestled along the Cilento Coast in southern Italy, Marina di Pisciotta is a charming fishing village with pristine beaches and crystalline waters. Explore secluded coves, enjoy fresh seafood at local trattorias, and soak up the laid-back atmosphere of this hidden gem.

Spiaggia delle Due Sorelle, Marche: Located near the town of Ancona on Italy's Adriatic coast, Spiaggia delle Due Sorelle (Beach of the Two Sisters) is a secluded beach with golden sand, rugged cliffs, and clear waters. Accessible via a steep staircase carved into the cliffs, this hidden gem offers stunning views and tranquillity away from the crowds.

Spiaggia di Sansone, Elba Island: Tucked away on the northern coast of Elba Island, Spiaggia di Sansone is a hidden paradise with crystal-clear waters, white pebble shores, and dramatic granite cliffs. Accessible via a short hike down a steep path, this secluded beach is perfect for swimming, snorkelling, and sunbathing.

Cala Pulcino, Puglia: Located in the Gargano Peninsula in Puglia, Cala Pulcino is a hidden gem with pristine turquoise waters, golden sand, and dramatic limestone cliffs. Accessible only by boat or a challenging hike, this secluded cove offers a tranquil escape from the crowds.

These secret beaches offer a chance to discover hidden treasures and enjoy the natural beauty of Italy's coastline away from the tourist crowds. Whether you're seeking secluded coves, pristine waters, or breathtaking scenery, these hidden gems are sure to provide unforgettable experiences and moments of serenity.

Hidden Culinary Delights

Exploring hidden culinary delights is a delightful way to uncover the authentic flavours and traditions of Italian cuisine. Here are some lesser-known culinary treasures worth discovering:

Cacio e Pepe in Rome: While Rome is famous for its pasta dishes like carbonara and amatriciana, don't miss the chance to try cacio e pepe, a simple yet delicious dish made with pasta, Pecorino Romano cheese, and black pepper. Head to local trattorias and osterias off the beaten path for a taste of this classic Roman favourite.

Focaccia in Liguria: Liguria is renowned for its savoury focaccia, a flatbread topped with olive oil, salt, and sometimes herbs or other toppings. Visit local bakeries and street markets in towns like Genoa and Camogli to sample different varieties of this traditional Ligurian snack.

Sarde a Beccafico in Sicily: In Sicily, don't miss the chance to try sarde a beccafico, a traditional dish made with fresh sardines stuffed with breadcrumbs, pine nuts, raisins, and herbs. Look for authentic trattorias and seafood restaurants in coastal towns like Palermo and Catania for a taste of this Sicilian delicacy.

Culurgiones in Sardinia: Culurgiones are traditional Sardinian stuffed pasta dumplings filled with a savoury mixture of potatoes, cheese, and herbs. Visit local agriturismo (farmhouse restaurants) and family-run trattorias in towns like Oliena and Orgosolo to savour this unique Sardinian specialty.

Frico in Friuli-Venezia Giulia: Frico is a traditional dish from the Friuli-Venezia Giulia region made with shredded cheese (usually Montasio) cooked until crispy. Look for frico served as an appetiser or side dish in rustic trattorias and agritourism throughout the region.

Orecchiette in Puglia: Puglia is famous for its orecchiette pasta, shaped like small ears, which is often served with traditional sauces like broccoli rabe and sausage or tomato and ricotta. Visit local pasta shops and family-run trattorias in towns like Bari and Lecce to sample this quintessential Puglian dish.

Baccalà Mantecato in Venice: Baccalà mantecato is a creamy spread made with salted cod, olive oil, garlic, and parsley, traditionally served on crostini as a Venetian appetiser. Look for authentic bacari (wine bars) and Cicchetti bars in Venice's hidden alleys and squares for a taste of this local specialty.

Ciccioli in Emilia-Romagna: Ciccioli are traditional pork cracklings popular in Emilia-

Romagna, made by slowly rendering pork fat until crispy. Visit local salumerie (delicatessens) and markets in towns like Modena and Parma to taste this savoury snack.

These hidden culinary delights offer a chance to discover the diverse flavours and regional specialties of Italian cuisine beyond the usual tourist spots. Whether you're exploring bustling cities, charming villages, or seaside towns, these hidden gems are sure to tantalise your taste buds and provide memorable gastronomic experiences.

Chapter 5

Historical Sites

Italy is a treasure trove of historical sites, spanning millennia of civilization. Here are some lesser-known historical gems worth exploring:

Paestum, Campania: Explore the well-preserved Greek ruins of Paestum, including three majestic Doric temples dating back to the 6th and 5th centuries BC. Wander among the ancient columns and admire the intricate details of these archaeological wonders.

Necropolis of Banditaccia, Lazio: Discover the UNESCO-listed Etruscan necropolis of Banditaccia in Cerveteri, near Rome. Explore the vast network of rock-cut tombs and tumuli dating back to the 9th century BC, offering insight into Etruscan burial customs and society.

Etruscan Tombs of Tarquinia, Lazio: Visit the Etruscan necropolis of Tarquinia, another UNESCO World Heritage Site, known for its painted tombs adorned with colourful frescoes depicting scenes of daily life, mythology, and rituals from the 6th to 3rd centuries BC.

Herculaneum, Campania: Explore the lesser-known sister city of Pompeii, Herculaneum, which was also buried by the eruption of Mount Vesuvius in 79 AD. Wander through the remarkably preserved streets, houses, and public buildings of this ancient Roman town frozen in time.

Ostia Antica, Lazio: Step back in time at Ostia Antica, the ancient port city of Rome located at the mouth of the Tiber River. Explore the well-preserved ruins of Ostia's streets, houses, temples, and amphitheatre, offering a glimpse into daily life in ancient Rome.

Alberobello Trulli, Apulia: Discover the unique trulli houses of Alberobello, a UNESCO World Heritage Site. These traditional dry-stone dwellings with conical roofs are found nowhere else in the world and offer a fascinating glimpse into the architectural heritage of the Apulia region.

Villa Romana del Casale, Sicily: Marvel at the well-preserved Roman mosaics of Villa Romana del Casale in Piazza Armerina, Sicily. Explore the ancient villa's opulent rooms adorned with intricate floor mosaics depicting scenes of mythology, hunting, and daily life.

Nuragic Complex of Barumini, Sardinia: Visit the UNESCO-listed Nuragic complex of Su Nuraxi in Barumini, Sardinia, dating back to the Bronze Age. Explore the central tower and surrounding village, which offer insight into the ancient Nuragic civilization that inhabited the island.

These lesser-known historical sites offer a fascinating glimpse into Italy's rich and diverse history, from ancient civilizations to mediaeval towns and Renaissance palaces. Whether you're exploring ancient ruins, archaeological sites, or architectural wonders, these hidden gems are sure to captivate and inspire visitors with their timeless beauty and cultural significance.

Ancient Rome

Ancient Rome, once the heart of one of the greatest empires in history, is rich in historical sites that offer a glimpse into its glorious past. Here are some lesser-known ancient Roman sites worth exploring:

Theatre of Marcellus: Built by Emperor Augustus in the 1st century BC, the Theatre of Marcellus is one of Rome's oldest and largest theatres. While it's not as well-known as the Colosseum or the Roman Forum, it's worth visiting for its impressive architecture and historical significance.

Baths of Caracalla: Explore the ruins of the Baths of Caracalla, one of ancient Rome's largest and most luxurious public bath complexes. Built in the 3rd century AD, the baths were a place for Romans to socialise, exercise, and relax in thermal pools and saunas.

Portus: Discover the ancient harbour of Portus, located just outside Rome near the modern town of Fiumicino. Built by Emperor Claudius in the 1st century AD, Portus was a vital hub for trade and commerce, connecting Rome to the Mediterranean world.

Ara Pacis Augustae: Admire the Ara Pacis Augustae, or Altar of Augustan Peace, a beautifully preserved monument dedicated to peace and prosperity during the reign of Emperor Augustus. Located near the Tiber River, the Ara Pacis is adorned with intricate reliefs depicting scenes of Roman life and mythology.

Domus Aurea: Explore the ruins of Emperor Nero's lavish Golden House, known as the Domus Aurea. Buried for centuries after Nero's death, the palace was rediscovered in the Renaissance and became a source of inspiration for artists such as Raphael and Michelangelo.

Appian Way: Walk along the ancient Appian Way, one of the oldest and most important Roman roads. Builtin 312 BC, the Appian Way connected Rome to the port city of Brindisi in southern Italy and played a crucial role in the expansion of the Roman Empire.

Circus Maximus: Visit the Circus Maximus, an ancient chariot racing stadium and entertainment venue located in the valley between the Palatine and Aventine Hills. While little remains of the original structure today, the site offers panoramic views of the surrounding area and a glimpse into ancient Roman life.

Tomb of Eurysaces the Baker: Marvel at the Tomb of Eurysaces the Baker, an unusual and well-preserved tomb dating back to the 1st century BC. Decorated with intricate reliefs depicting scenes from the baker's life and trade, the tomb offers a fascinating glimpse into ancient Roman funerary practices.

These lesser-known ancient Roman sites offer a unique opportunity to explore the city's rich history and archaeological heritage beyond the well-trodden paths of the Colosseum and the Roman Forum. Whether you're interested in ancient architecture, imperial monuments, or everyday life in ancient Rome, these hidden gems are sure to captivate and inspire visitors with their timeless beauty and historical significance.

Renaissance Florence

During the Renaissance, Florence flourished as a center of art, culture, and intellectual thought, attracting some of the greatest artists, thinkers, and patrons of the time. Here are some lesser-known aspects of Renaissance Florence worth exploring:

Palazzo Davanzati: Step back in time at Palazzo Davanzati, a mediaeval palace that offers a glimpse into the daily life of Renaissance-era Florentine nobility. Explore the beautifully preserved rooms, courtyards, and decorative arts collections, including furniture, textiles, and ceramics.

Bargello Museum: Discover the Bargello Museum, housed in a former mediaeval palace, which showcases a superb collection of Renaissance sculpture and decorative arts. Admire masterpieces by artists such as Donatello, Michelangelo, and Cellini, as well as exquisite examples of Renaissance metalwork and ceramics.

Medici Chapels: Visit the Medici Chapels, located within the Basilica of San Lorenzo, to see the mausoleums of the powerful Medici family. Admire the elegant architecture and marble sculptures by Michelangelo, including the famous Medici Tombs, which are among the artist's finest works.

Orsanmichele Church: Explore the Orsanmichele Church, a unique blend of religious and civic architecture that was once a grain market and guildhall. Admire the intricate tabernacles on the exterior, each housing a statue of a patron saint created by leading Renaissance artists such as Donatello and Ghiberti.

Leonardo da Vinci Museum: Delve into the world of Leonardo da Vinci at the Leonardo da Vinci Museum, located near the Uffizi Gallery. Explore interactive exhibits and reconstructions of Leonardo's inventions, scientific studies, and artistic techniques, providing insight into the mind of the Renaissance polymath.

Villa Medicea di Castello: Escape the crowds of the city and visit the Villa Medicea di Castello, a Renaissance villa located in the hills outside Florence. Explore the villa's gardens, terraces, and frescoed interiors, which were once the summer retreat of the Medici family.

San Marco Museum: Visit the San Marco Museum, housed in a former Dominican monastery, to see the frescoes of Fra Angelico, one of the greatest painters of the early Renaissance. Admire the serene beauty of Angelico's masterpieces, including his famous Annunciation and Crucifixion scenes.

Vasari Corridor: Embark on a private tour of the Vasari Corridor, a secret passageway built by the Medici family in the 16th century. Walk in the footsteps of Renaissance luminaries as you follow the corridor from the Palazzo Vecchio, through the Uffizi Gallery, to the Pitti Palace, enjoying panoramic views of the city along the way.

These lesser-known aspects of Renaissance Florence offer a deeper understanding of the city's artistic legacy and cultural heritage, providing a fascinating glimpse into one of the most vibrant periods in history. Whether you're exploring hidden museums, admiring Renaissance sculpture, or strolling through historic gardens, these hidden gems are sure to enrich your experience of Florence's Renaissance treasures.

Medieval Hilltop Towns

Exploring mediaeval hilltop towns is like stepping back in time to a bygone era of cobblestone streets, ancient fortifications, and panoramic views of the surrounding countryside. Here are some lesser-known mediaeval hilltop towns worth discovering in Italy:

Montefioralle, Tuscany: Tucked away in the heart of Chianti wine country, Montefioralle is a picturesque mediaeval village surrounded by vineyards and olive groves. Explore its narrow streets, mediaeval walls, and well-preserved architecture, including the 12th-century Church of Santo Stefano.

Vigoleno, Emilia-Romagna: Perched atop a hill in the Emilia-Romagna region, Vigoleno is a fortified village with a rich history dating back to the Middle Ages. Wander through its labyrinthine streets, visit the imposing castle, and enjoy breathtaking views of the surrounding countryside.

Moresco, Marche: With its charming stone houses, mediaeval walls, and panoramic views of the Adriatic Sea, Moresco is a hidden gem in the Marche region. Explore its well-preserved historic centre, visit the 14th-century Church of San Nicola, and soak up the atmosphere of this timeless village.

Castell'Arquato, Emilia-Romagna:

Surrounded by vineyards and rolling hills, Castell'Arquato is a mediaeval jewel in the Emilia-Romagna countryside. Admire its well-preserved mediaeval architecture, including the imposing Visconti Castle and the Romanesque Cathedral of Santa Maria Assunta.

Monselice, Veneto:

Nestled in the Euganean Hills near Padua, Monselice is a mediaeval town with a rich history and stunning views of the surrounding landscape. Explore its mediaeval walls, historic palaces, and picturesque gardens, including the scenic Villa Duodo-Martinengo.

Sant'Agata Feltria, Emilia-Romagna:

Set amidst the rolling hills of the Montefeltro region, Sant'Agata Feltria is a charming mediaeval town known for its well-preserved historic centre and annual truffle festival. Explore its winding streets, visit the mediaeval fortress, and enjoy panoramic views of the Apennine Mountains.

Castel del Monte, Apulia:

Perched atop a hill in the Apulian countryside, Castel del Monte is a

UNESCO World Heritage Site renowned for its unique octagonal shape and mediaeval architecture. Explore its mysterious interior, adorned with intricate stone carvings and geometric patterns.

Civita di Bagnoregio, Lazio: Known as the "dying town," Civita di Bagnoregio is a mediaeval hilltop village perched atop a tufa rock plateau in the Lazio region. Accessible only by a pedestrian bridge, Civita di Bagnoregio offers a glimpse into Italy's mediaeval past and breathtaking views of the surrounding countryside.

These lesser-known mediaeval hilltop towns offer a glimpse into Italy's rich history, architectural heritage, and cultural traditions. Whether you're exploring ancient fortresses, wandering through cobblestone streets, or admiring panoramic views, these hidden gems are sure to enchant and inspire visitors with their timeless beauty and romantic ambiance.

Chapter 6

Cultural Experiences

Exploring cultural experiences in Italy offers a deeper understanding of the country's rich heritage and diverse traditions. Here are some lesser-known cultural experiences worth discovering:

Truffle Hunting in Piedmont: Join a truffle hunter and his trained dog in the forests of Piedmont for a unique culinary adventure. Learn about the art of truffle hunting, sample fresh truffles, and enjoy a traditional Piedmontese meal paired with local wines.

Traditional Mask Making in Venice: Discover the ancient art of mask making in Venice by participating in a workshop with a local artisan. Learn about the history and symbolism of Venetian masks, and create your masterpiece using traditional techniques and materials.

Cheese Making in Emilia-Romagna: Visit a family-run cheese dairy in Emilia-Romagna to learn the secrets of traditional Italian cheese making. Get hands-on experience crafting Parmigiano Reggiano or other local cheeses, and taste the fruits of your labour paired with regional wines and gourmet specialties.

Olive Oil Tasting in Tuscany: Experience the flavours of Tuscany by participating in an olive oil tasting tour at a local farm or olive grove. Learn about the cultivation and production of extra virgin olive oil, sample different varieties, and discover the nuances of this essential ingredient in Italian cuisine.

Ceramic Painting in Umbria: Unleash your creativity by painting your ceramic masterpiece in the picturesque town of Deruta, known for its centuries-old tradition of ceramic craftsmanship. Join a workshop with a local artisan to learn the techniques of ceramic painting and create your unique souvenir to take home.

Gondola Building in Venice: Discover the ancient art of gondola building by visiting a traditional boatyard, or "square," in Venice. Witness skilled craftsmen at work as they construct and repair these iconic wooden boats using time-honoured techniques passed down through generations.

Traditional Weaving in Sardinia: Explore the ancient craft of traditional weaving in Sardinia by visiting a local workshop or museum dedicated to textile arts. Learn about the intricate patterns and techniques used to create Sardinian textiles, and perhaps try your hand at weaving your souvenir.

Falconry in Tuscany: Embark on a falconry experience in the Tuscan countryside, where you can learn about the ancient art of falconry and witness majestic birds of prey in flight. Participate in a falconry demonstration, handle trained raptors, and gain insight into this fascinating aspect of Italian cultural heritage.

These lesser-known cultural experiences offer a unique opportunity to immerse yourself in Italy's rich traditions, artisanal crafts, and culinary delights. Whether you're learning a traditional craft, sampling local delicacies, or exploring ancient traditions, these hidden gems are sure to leave you with lasting memories and a deeper appreciation for Italian culture.

Art and Architecture

Exploring the art and architecture of Italy is like stepping into a living museum filled with masterpieces from different periods and styles. Here are some lesser-known art and architectural treasures worth discovering:

San Miniato al Monte, Florence: Perched atop a hill overlooking Florence, San Miniato al Monte is a Romanesque gem known for its stunning architecture and exquisite marble facade. Admire the intricate geometric patterns, sculptures, and mosaic work that adorn this 11th-century basilica.

Palazzo Schifanoia, Ferrara: Explore the Palazzo Schifanoia in Ferrara, a Renaissance palace renowned for its magnificent frescoes depicting scenes from classical mythology, astrology, and the life of the ruling Este family. Marvel at the intricate details and vibrant colours of these 15th-century masterpieces.

Santa Maria della Vittoria, Rome: Visit the Santa Maria della Vittoria church in Rome to see one of Gian Lorenzo Bernini's lesser-known masterpieces, the Ecstasy of Saint Teresa. Marvel at the dramatic sculpture of Saint Teresa in a state of divine rapture, illuminated by golden light streaming through the chapel's windows.

Villa Farnese, Caprarola: Discover the Villa Farnese in Caprarola, a stunning Renaissance villa surrounded by lush gardens and terraced landscapes. Explore the palace's lavishly decorated rooms, including the Sala dei Fasti Farnesiani, adorned with frescoes depicting the glory of the Farnese family.

Church of San Francesco, Arezzo: Admire the frescoes of Piero della Francesca in the Church of San Francesco in Arezzo, a UNESCO World Heritage Site. Marvel at the artist's masterful use of perspective and light in works such as the Legend of the True Cross fresco cycle.

Palazzo dei Normanni, Palermo: Visit the Palazzo dei Normanni in Palermo to see the stunning Palatine Chapel, a masterpiece of Arab-Norman architecture and one of the most important examples of mediaeval art in Italy. Admire the intricate mosaics, marble columns, and muqarnas ceiling, reflecting the cultural fusion of Sicily's past.

Villa Borghese Gardens, Rome: Escape the hustle and bustle of Rome and explore the Villa Borghese Gardens, a vast park filled with sculptures, fountains, and neoclassical architecture. Discover hidden gems such as the Temple of Aesculapius, the Pincian Hill overlook, and the picturesque lake.

Palazzo Spada, Rome: Step into the Baroque world of Francesco Borromini at Palazzo Spada in

Rome. Admire the architect's trompe-l'oeil masterpiece, the Borromini Perspective Gallery, which creates the illusion of a long corridor in a small space using forced perspective.

These lesser-known art and architectural treasures offer a deeper appreciation of Italy's rich cultural heritage and the enduring legacy of its artistic masters. Whether you're exploring hidden churches, palaces, or gardens, these hidden gems are sure to inspire and captivate visitors with their beauty and historical significance.

Music and Opera

Italy has a rich musical heritage, and experiencing music and opera in this country is a cultural treat. Here are some lesser-known music and opera experiences worth exploring:

Ravello Festival, Amalfi Coast: Enjoy the Ravello Festival, a renowned music festival held annually in the picturesque town of Ravello on the

Amalfi Coast. Set against the backdrop of stunning coastal views, the festival features performances by renowned musicians, orchestras, and opera singers in historic venues such as Villa Rufolo and Villa Cimbrone.

Teatro La Fenice, Venice: Attend a performance at Teatro La Fenice, one of Italy's most prestigious opera houses, located in the heart of Venice. Built in the 18th century, La Fenice has a rich history and has hosted premieres of operas by composers such as Verdi, Rossini, and Donizetti.

Rossini Opera Festival, Pesaro: Immerse yourself in the world of opera at the Rossini Opera Festival, held annually in the composer's hometown of Pesaro. Celebrating the works of Gioachino Rossini, the festival features performances of his operas, as well as concerts, recitals, and lectures.

Maggio Musicale Fiorentino, Florence: Experience the Maggio Musicale Fiorentino, one of Italy's oldest and most prestigious music festivals, held annually in Florence. Founded in 1933, the festival features a diverse program of opera, concerts, ballet, and chamber music, attracting top performers from around the world.

Verdi Festival, Parma: Discover the Verdi Festival, held annually in the composer's hometown of Parma to celebrate the works of Giuseppe Verdi. Experience performances of Verdi's operas in historic venues such as the Teatro Regio and the Teatro Farnese, as well as concerts, exhibitions, and lectures.

Arena di Verona, Verona: Attend a performance at the Arena di Verona, an ancient Roman amphitheatre that hosts opera productions during the summer months. Experience the magic of opera under the stars in this historic venue, which has a seating capacity of over 15,000 spectators.

Santa Cecilia Conservatory, Rome: Enjoy a concert at the Santa Cecilia Conservatory in Rome, one of the oldest and most prestigious music institutions in the world. Founded in the 16th century, the conservatory hosts regular performances by students, faculty, and guest artists in a variety of genres, from classical to contemporary.

Sferisterio Opera Festival, Macerata:
Experience opera in a unique setting at the Sferisterio Opera Festival in Macerata, held in an open-air arena originally built for a traditional Italian ball game. Enjoy performances of opera classics in this historic venue, which offers excellent acoustics and panoramic views of the surrounding countryside.

These lesser-known music and opera experiences offer a chance to immerse yourself in Italy's rich musical heritage and cultural traditions, whether you're attending a festival, concert, or opera performance. With its historic venues, world-class performers, and diverse programming, Italy is a paradise for music lovers and opera enthusiasts alike.

Festivals and Events

Italy is renowned for its vibrant festivals and events, celebrating everything from art and music to food and culture. Here are some lesser-known festivals and events worth experiencing:

Infiorata di Noto, Sicily: Witness the stunning floral carpets of the Infiorata di Noto, held annually in the town of Noto in southeastern Sicily. During this three-day event, the streets of Noto are adorned with intricate designs made from thousands of flower petals, creating a colourful tapestry that celebrates springtime and religious traditions.

Sagra del Mandorlo in Fiore, Sicily: Experience the almond blossom festival, known as the Sagra del Mandorlo in Fiore, in Agrigento, Sicily. Held in February, this festival celebrates the beauty of the almond trees in bloom with parades, concerts, traditional music, and food stalls offering almond-based delicacies.

Festa della Sensa, Venice: Join the Festa della Sensa, a traditional Venetian festival celebrating the city's maritime heritage and relationship with the sea. Held annually on Ascension Day, the festival includes a symbolic marriage ceremony between Venice and the Adriatic Sea, as well as boat parades, regattas, and cultural events.

Palio di Asti, Piedmont: Experience the historic horse race of the Palio di Asti, held annually in the city of Asti in Piedmont. Dating back to the 13th century, this thrilling event features jockeys representing different districts of Asti competing in a high-speed race around the city's historic Piazza Alfieri.

Festival of the Ceri, Umbria: Witness the Festival of the Ceri, a traditional event held annually in Gubbio, Umbria, to honour the city's patron saint, Saint Ubaldo. During the festival, three massive wooden ceri (candles) representing the city's three patron saints are carried through the streets in a spectacular procession accompanied by flag-waving and mediaeval pageantry.

Sagra del Redentore, Venice: Celebrate the Sagra del Redentore, a traditional Venetian festival held in July to commemorate the end of the plague in the 16th century. The highlight of the festival is a spectacular fireworks display over the waters of the Venetian lagoon, accompanied by boat processions, feasting, and live music.

Festival of Sant'Efisio, Sardinia: Experience the Festival of Sant'Efisio, one of the most important religious and cultural events in Sardinia, held annually in Cagliari. The festival honours the martyr Saint Efisio with a colourful procession featuring traditional costumes, folk music, and horse-drawn carts, culminating in a pilgrimage to the church of Nora.

Carnival of Ivrea, Piedmont: Discover the historic Carnival of Ivrea, a unique event featuring the traditional "Battle of the Oranges." Participants divide into teams representing historical factions and engage in a spirited orange-throwing battle through the streets of Ivrea, commemorating a mediaeval uprising against tyrannical rulers.

These lesser-known festivals and events offer a glimpse into Italy's rich cultural heritage and provide unforgettable experiences for travellers seeking to immerse themselves in local traditions and celebrations. Whether you're witnessing ancient rituals, enjoying culinary delights, or participating in historic reenactments, these hidden gems are sure to leave a lasting impression and create cherished memories of your time in Italy.

Chapter 7

Outdoor Adventures

Italy's diverse landscapes offer a wealth of outdoor adventures for nature lovers and thrill-seekers alike. Here are some lesser-known outdoor adventures worth exploring:

Hiking in the Cinque Terre: Explore the scenic trails of the Cinque Terre National Park, a UNESCO World Heritage Site located along the rugged coastline of the Italian Riviera. Hike along ancient footpaths that connect the five colourful villages of Monterosso al Mare, Vernazza, Corniglia, Manarola, and Riomaggiore, and enjoy breathtaking views of the Mediterranean Sea.

Rock Climbing in Finale Ligure: Discover the world-class rock climbing destination of Finale Ligure, located on the Ligurian coast near Genoa. Climb limestone cliffs overlooking the sea, with routes suitable for climbers of all levels, and enjoy stunning views of the coastline and surrounding countryside.

Cycling in the Dolomites: Explore the dramatic landscapes of the Dolomites by bike, pedalling along scenic mountain roads and thrilling descents. Cycle through charming alpine villages, past sparkling lakes, and beneath towering peaks, and experience the beauty of this UNESCO World Heritage Site from a unique perspective.

Sea Kayaking in Sardinia: Paddle along the rugged coastline of Sardinia on a sea kayaking adventure, exploring hidden coves, sea caves, and pristine beaches. Navigate crystal-clear waters teeming with marine life, and discover secluded spots accessible only by kayak, away from the crowds of the mainland.

Wildlife Watching in Abruzzo National Park: Embark on a wildlife-watching excursion in Abruzzo National Park, one of Italy's largest and most biodiverse protected areas. Keep an eye out for native species such as Marsican brown bears, Apennine wolves, and Abruzzo chamois as you hike through beech forests, alpine meadows, and mountainous terrain.

Ski Touring in the Gran Paradiso National Park: Experience the thrill of ski touring in the Gran Paradiso National Park, located in the western Italian Alps near the border with France. Explore remote valleys, high-altitude glaciers, and pristine powder slopes on a guided ski expedition, and enjoy breathtaking views of the surrounding peaks.

Stand-Up Paddleboarding on Lake Garda: Glide across the turquoise waters of Lake Garda on a stand-up paddleboarding excursion, exploring hidden coves, mediaeval castles, and picturesque villages along the shoreline. Enjoy the tranquillity of the lake and soak up the Mediterranean sun as you paddle beneath towering cliffs and lush olive groves.

Caving in the Apuan Alps: Discover the underground world of the Apuan Alps on a caving adventure in Tuscany. Explore labyrinthine caves, underground rivers, and spectacular rock formations with experienced guides, and learn about the geological history and natural wonders of this unique karst landscape.

These lesser-known outdoor adventures offer a thrilling way to experience Italy's natural beauty and diverse landscapes, from coastal cliffs and alpine peaks to verdant forests and crystal-clear waters. Whether you're hiking, climbing, cycling, or paddling, these hidden gems are sure to provide unforgettable experiences and moments of exhilaration in the great outdoors.

Hiking in the Dolomites

Hiking in the Dolomites offers a spectacular way to immerse yourself in the stunning landscapes of this UNESCO World Heritage Site. Here are some lesser-known hiking trails worth exploring:

Val di Funes: Discover the beauty of Val di Funes, a picturesque valley dotted with charming villages and surrounded by towering peaks. Hike along scenic trails such as the Adolf Munkel Trail, which offers panoramic views of the Odle Group and the iconic Church of St. Magdalena.

Val Gardena: Explore the breathtaking landscapes of Val Gardena, known for its lush meadows, rugged cliffs, and vibrant alpine flora. Hike along the Panorama Trail, which winds through the Puez-Odle Nature Park, offering stunning views of the Sella Group and the Marmolada Glacier.

Val di Fassa: Wander through the enchanting valleys of Val di Fassa, home to some of the Dolomites' most iconic peaks, including the Catinaccio and the Sella Group. Hike the Roda de Vael Trail, a circular route that leads to the foot of the towering Vajolet Towers, surrounded by dramatic cliffs and alpine meadows.

Alta Badia: Explore the alpine paradise of Alta Badia, nestled beneath the towering peaks of the Sella Group and the Marmolada Glacier. Hike along the Piz Sorega Trail, which takes you through lush forests and pastures to panoramic viewpoints overlooking the Dolomite mountains.

Tre Cime di Lavaredo: Marvel at the iconic Tre Cime di Lavaredo, a trio of towering peaks that dominate the landscape of the Sexten Dolomites. Hike the Tre Cime Loop Trail, which offers breathtaking views of the jagged rock formations and the surrounding alpine scenery.

Valle del Bios: Discover the hidden gem of Valle del Bios, a pristine valley located in the heart of the Dolomites. Hike along the Sentiero del Bios, a scenic trail that follows the course of the Biois River, passing through lush forests, alpine meadows, and charming mountain villages.

Valle di Casies: Immerse yourself in the tranquillity of Valle di Casies, a secluded valley surrounded by rugged peaks and pristine wilderness. Hike the Casies Valley Trail, which winds through peaceful forests and meadows, offering glimpses of traditional alpine farmhouses and grazing cattle.

Val Pusteria: Explore the picturesque valleys of Val Pusteria, known for their rolling hills, lush pastures, and traditional Tyrolean villages. Hike along the Rienza River Trail, which follows the course of the river through scenic gorges and past cascading waterfalls, offering opportunities for wildlife spotting and birdwatching.

These lesser-known hiking trails in the Dolomites offer a chance to experience the beauty and tranquillity of this UNESCO World Heritage Site away from the crowds, surrounded by breathtaking scenery and pristine wilderness. Whether you're seeking panoramic views, alpine meadows, or dramatic rock formations, these hidden gems are sure to provide unforgettable hiking experiences in one of Europe's most stunning mountain ranges.

Cycling in Tuscany

Cycling in Tuscany offers a fantastic way to explore the region's picturesque countryside, charming villages, and historic towns. Here are some lesser-known cycling routes worth discovering:

Val d'Orcia: Pedal through the rolling hills and vineyards of Val d'Orcia, a UNESCO World Heritage Site renowned for its scenic beauty and cultural significance. Cycle along the Strada di Val d'Orcia, a winding road that connects the charming towns of Pienza, Montalcino, and Montepulciano, offering panoramic views of the countryside and iconic landmarks such as the Pienza Cathedral and the Sant'Antimo Abbey.

Garfagnana: Explore the rugged landscapes of Garfagnana, a mountainous region nestled between the Apuan Alps and the Tuscan-Emilian Apennines. Cycle along the Garfagnana Loop, a scenic route that winds through picturesque villages, chestnut forests, and mediaeval castles, offering breathtaking views of the surrounding mountains and valleys.

Maremma: Discover the coastal beauty of Maremma, a pristine region located along the southern coast of Tuscany. Cycle along the

Maremma Coastal Route, which follows quiet country roads and coastal trails from the historic town of Grosseto to the scenic beaches of Monte Argentario, passing through lush pine forests, sandy dunes, and charming seaside villages along the way.

Chianti: Pedal through the vineyards and olive groves of Chianti, one of Tuscany's most iconic wine regions. Cycle along the Chianti Classico Route, a scenic loop that winds through the rolling hills and mediaeval villages of the Chianti countryside, offering opportunities to visit wineries, sample local wines, and enjoy panoramic views of the vineyard-covered landscape.

Val di Chiana: Explore the fertile valley of Val di Chiana, located between the towns of Arezzo and Montepulciano. Cycle along the Val di Chiana Cycle Path, a flat and scenic route that follows the course of the Canale Maestro della Chiana, passing through picturesque countryside, sunflower fields, and historic villages such as Cortona and Lucignano.

Colline Metallifere: Discover the rugged beauty of the Colline Metallifere, a mountain range located in southern Tuscany near the border with Lazio. Cycle along the Colline Metallifere Loop, a challenging route that traverses steep hills, dense forests, and remote hilltop villages, offering stunning views of the surrounding countryside and the Tyrrhenian Sea in the distance.

Monti Pisani: Climb the scenic Monti Pisani, a mountain range located near the city of Pisa, and enjoy panoramic views of the Tuscan countryside and the nearby Ligurian Sea. Cycle along the Monti Pisani Circuit, a challenging route that takes you through chestnut forests, olive groves, and ancient villages, offering opportunities to explore historic landmarks such as the Certosa di Calci monastery and the village of San Giuliano Terme.

Crete Senesi: Experience the surreal landscapes of the Crete Senesi, a region characterised by rolling clay hills, cypress trees, and mediaeval villages. Cycle along the Crete Senesi Ring Route, a scenic loop that winds through the heart of this unique landscape, offering breathtaking views of the iconic scenery and the distant skyline of Siena.

These lesser-known cycling routes in Tuscany offer a chance to experience the region's natural beauty, cultural heritage, and culinary delights from a unique perspective. Whether you're exploring vineyard-covered hills, coastal landscapes, or mountainous terrain, these hidden gems are sure to provide unforgettable cycling adventures in one of Italy's most enchanting regions.

Sailing along the Amalfi Coast

Sailing along the Amalfi Coast offers a magical way to experience one of Italy's most breathtaking coastal landscapes. Here are some lesser-known highlights and tips for your sailing adventure:

Maiori and Minori: Start your sailing journey from the charming towns of Maiori and Minori, located at the eastern end of the Amalfi Coast. Explore their colourful harbours, historic architecture, and sandy beaches before setting sail along the rugged coastline.

Conca dei Marini: Cruise past the picturesque village of Conca dei Marini, nestled between cliffs and the azure waters of the Tyrrhenian Sea. Admire the iconic Grotta dello Smeraldo (Emerald Grotto), a stunning sea cave known for its emerald-coloured waters and dazzling stalactites.

Fiordo di Furore: Sail into the dramatic Fiordo di Furore, a deep fjord-like gorge carved into the cliffs of the Amalfi Coast. Marvel at the natural beauty of this hidden gem, which is home to a small beach and a charming fishing village suspended above the sea.

Praiano: Discover the coastal town of Praiano, known for its picturesque setting and laid-back atmosphere. Drop anchor in the sheltered cove of Marina di Praia and explore the quaint streets, historic churches, and panoramic viewpoints overlooking the sea.

Marina di Cetara: Visit the fishing village of Cetara and its charming marina, where colorful fishing boats bob in the water against the backdrop of pastel-coloured houses. Sample local delicacies such as anchovies, tuna, and colatura di alici (anchovy sauce) at one of the town's traditional trattorias.

Nerano: Anchor in the tranquil bay of Nerano and take a dip in the crystal-clear waters of the Baia di Ieranto, a protected marine area known for its pristine beaches and underwater caves. Enjoy a leisurely lunch at a waterfront restaurant, savouring fresh seafood and regional specialties.

Villa Rufolo and Villa Cimbrone: Admire the historic villas of Villa Rufolo and Villa Cimbrone from the sea, perched on the cliffs above the town of Ravello. Marvel at their lush gardens, ornate architecture, and panoramic views of the coastline, and imagine the glamorous parties and cultural gatherings that once took place within their walls.

Positano: End your sailing adventure in the iconic town of Positano, with its colourful buildings cascading down the cliffs to the sea. Explore the narrow streets, boutique shops, and cliffside cafes of this picturesque village before bidding farewell to the enchanting Amalfi Coast.

When sailing along the Amalfi Coast, be sure to check weather conditions and sea currents, especially in the summer months when the sea can be choppy and crowded with other vessels. Consider hiring a local skipper or joining a guided sailing tour to make the most of your experience and discover hidden coves and secret beaches inaccessible by land. With its stunning scenery, charming villages, and crystalline waters, sailing along the Amalfi Coast promises an unforgettable adventure and memories to last a lifetime.

Chapter 8

Culinary Delights

Exploring the culinary delights of Italy is a gastronomic adventure filled with flavours, traditions, and regional specialties. Here are some lesser-known culinary experiences worth savouring:

Cucina Povera in Puglia: Discover the rustic simplicity of Puglian cuisine, known as Cucina Povera, which celebrates humble ingredients and traditional cooking methods. Sample dishes such as orecchiette with turnip greens, fava bean puree, and Frisella bread topped with tomatoes and olive oil, and savour the flavours of this authentic southern Italian cuisine.

Ligurian Sea Food in Camogli: Indulge in the fresh seafood of Liguria in the picturesque fishing village of Camogli, located along the Italian Riviera. Feast on local specialties such as stuffed anchovies, seafood risotto, and trofie pasta with pesto, paired with crisp Ligurian wines and stunning views of the Mediterranean Sea.

Sicilian Street Food in Palermo: Immerse yourself in the vibrant street food culture of Palermo, Sicily's capital city, and sample an array of traditional snacks and delicacies from local markets and street vendors. Taste arancini (rice balls), panelle (chickpea fritters), sfincione (Sicilian pizza), and cannoli (ricotta-filled pastries), and experience the flavours of Sicily's diverse culinary heritage.

Alpine Cuisine in South Tyrol: Explore the alpine cuisine of South Tyrol, a region nestled in the Dolomites near the Austrian border. Enjoy hearty dishes such as speck dumplings, käsespätzle (cheese noodles), and apple strudel, influenced by both Italian and Austrian culinary traditions, and accompanied by local beers and schnapps.

Truffle Hunting in Umbria: Join a truffle hunting excursion in the forests of Umbria, known as the "green heart" of Italy, and discover the secrets of this prized culinary delicacy. Follow trained truffle dogs as they sniff out the elusive fungi hidden beneath the forest floor, and enjoy a truffle-themed feast featuring pasta, risotto, and cheese infused with the rich, earthy flavours of black and white truffles.

Artisanal Cheeses in Piedmont: Delight your taste buds with the artisanal cheeses of Piedmont, a region renowned for its dairy products and culinary traditions. Sample varieties such as Castelmagno, Robiola, and Toma Piemontese, paired with local honey, fruit preserves, and freshly baked bread, and learn about the centuries-old cheese-making techniques passed down through generations.

Venetian Cicchetti in Venice: Experience the culinary tradition of Cicchetti in Venice, small plates of savoury snacks and appetisers served in traditional bacari (wine bars) throughout the city. Enjoy a leisurely cicchetti crawl, sampling dishes such as baccalà mantecato (whipped salt cod), sarde in saor (marinated sardines), and polpette (meatballs), accompanied by a glass of local wine or spritz.

Sardinian Suckling Pig in Nuoro: Feast on the traditional delicacy of Sardinian suckling pig, known as "***proceeds***," in the town of Nuoro, located in the heart of the island. Savour tender roasted pork infused with aromatic herbs and spices, served with crispy crackling skin and accompanied by traditional Sardinian sides such as pane carasau (crisp flatbread) and cannon as wine.

These lesser-known culinary experiences offer a taste of Italy's diverse culinary heritage, from the rustic flavours of the south to the alpine specialties of the north. Whether you're sampling street food in Sicily, truffle hunting in Umbria, or enjoying cicchetti in Venice, these hidden gems are sure to delight your senses and leave you craving more of Italy's culinary delights.

Regional Cuisine

Exploring regional cuisine in Italy is like embarking on a culinary journey through diverse landscapes, traditions, and flavours. Here are some lesser-known regional cuisines worth savouring:

Friuli-Venezia Giulia: Discover the unique blend of Italian, Austrian, and Slovenian influences in the cuisine of Friuli-Venezia Giulia, a northeastern region bordering Austria and Slovenia. Indulge in dishes such as frico (a crispy cheese and potato pancake), jota (a hearty bean and sauerkraut soup), and Guyana (a sweet pastry filled with nuts, fruit, and spices), and sample local wines such as Friulano and Ribolla Gialla.

Le Marche: Taste the flavours of Le Marche, a central region known for its rolling hills, olive groves, and Adriatic coastline. Enjoy dishes such as vincisgrassi (a rich lasagna-style pasta dish), brodetto (a savoury fish stew), and olive all'ascolana (stuffed olives), and savour regional wines such as Verdicchio and Rosso Conero.

Abruzzo: Explore the hearty cuisine of Abruzzo, a mountainous region located in central Italy known for its rugged landscapes and traditional mountain fare. Feast on dishes such as arrosticini (grilled lamb skewers), maccheroni alla chitarra (handmade pasta served with a rich tomato sauce), and confetti di Sulmona (sugared almonds), and enjoy robust wines such as Montepulciano d'Abruzzo and Trebbiano d'Abruzzo.

Molise: Experience the rustic cuisine of Molise, one of Italy's smallest and least-visited regions, located between Abruzzo and Puglia. Sample dishes such as cavatelli molisani (handmade pasta with tomato sauce and pecorino cheese), riso e patate (rice and potato soup), and bocconotti (pastry filled with chocolate and almonds), and taste local wines such as Tintilia del Molise and Aglianico del Molise.

Basilicata: Delight in the flavours of Basilicata, a southern region known for its rugged landscapes, ancient traditions, and hearty cuisine. Enjoy dishes such as pepperoni crunchy (crispy fried peppers), ciaudedda (a vegetable and bean stew), and lagane e ceci (handmade pasta with chickpeas), and savor regional wines such as Aglianico del Vulture and Matera Bianco.

Calabria: Explore the bold flavours of Calabria, the toe of Italy's boot, known for its spicy peppers, citrus fruits, and seafood. Indulge in dishes such as nduja (spicy spreadable salami), Sardella (anchovy paste), and swordfish involtini (swordfish rolls), and sample regional wines such as Cirò and Greco di Bianco.

Valle d'Aosta: Experience the alpine cuisine of Valle d'Aosta, a mountainous region nestled in the western Italian Alps near the borders of France and Switzerland. Enjoy dishes such as fondue (a creamy cheese fondue), carbonade Valdosta (a beef stew with red wine and polenta), and tartiflette (a potato and cheese gratin), and savour local wines such as Petite Arvine and Nebbiolo.

Sardinia: Taste the flavours of Sardinia, an island located off the coast of southern Italy known for its pristine beaches, rugged interior, and ancient culinary traditions. Feast on dishes such as culurgiones (stuffed pasta), proceeds (suckling pig roasted on a spit), and sedans (a pastry filled with cheese and honey), and enjoy regional wines such as Cannonau and Vermentino.

These lesser-known regional cuisines offer a glimpse into Italy's diverse culinary heritage, showcasing the unique ingredients, flavours, and traditions of each distinct area. Whether you're exploring the mountain villages of Abruzzo, the coastal towns of Le Marche, or the rugged landscapes of Basilicata, these hidden gems are sure to delight your taste buds and leave you craving more of Italy's culinary delights.

Wine Tasting

Wine tasting in Italy is a delightful journey through centuries of winemaking tradition, diverse terroirs, and exquisite flavours. Here are some lesser-known wine regions and experiences worth exploring:

Lombardy - Franciacorta: Discover the sparkling wines of Franciacorta, a region located in the province of Brescia in Lombardy. Known as Italy's answer to Champagne, Franciacorta produces elegant and nuanced sparkling wines using the traditional method. Visit boutique wineries such as Ca' del Bosco, Bellavista, and Ferghettina to taste their Franciacorta wines and explore the picturesque vineyards.

Trentino-Alto Adige - Alto Adige: Explore the Alpine wines of Alto Adige, a region nestled in the foothills of the Dolomites in Trentino-Alto Adige. Sample crisp white wines such as Pinot Grigio, Gewürztraminer, and Müller-Thurgau, as well as elegant reds like Lagrein and Schiava. Visit family-owned wineries in villages such as Bolzano, Caldaro, and Merano to taste the wines and enjoy stunning mountain views.

Friuli-Venezia Giulia - Collio: Experience the aromatic wines of Collio, a subregion of Friuli-Venezia Giulia known for its white wines made from grapes such as Friulano, Ribolla Gialla, and Malvasia. Taste the unique expressions of terroir in wines from renowned producers such as Ronco del Gnemiz, Edi Keber, and Livio Felluga, and enjoy guided tastings paired with local cheeses, prosciutto, and olive oil.

Campania - Irpinia: Explore the volcanic wines of Irpinia, a subregion of Campania known for its indigenous grape varieties and mineral-rich soils. Taste bold red wines such as Aglianico and Taurasi, as well as crisp whites like Fiano and Greco di Tufo, at wineries such as Mastroberardino, Feudi di San Gregorio, and Terredora di Paolo. Visit vineyards nestled among the rolling hills and ancient villages of Irpinia to learn about the region's winemaking traditions and history.

Sicily - Etna: Discover the volcanic wines of Mount Etna, a UNESCO World Heritage Site located on the east coast of Sicily. Taste elegant red wines made from Nerello Mascalese and Nerello Cappuccio grapes grown on the slopes of Europe's highest active volcano, as well as crisp whites from Carricante and Catarratto. Visit boutique wineries such as Benanti, Pietradolce, and Passopisciaro to taste the wines and enjoy panoramic views of the Mediterranean Sea.

Piedmont - Roero: Explore the elegant wines of Roero, a subregion of Piedmont known for its red wines made from Nebbiolo and white wines from Arneis. Taste the complex flavours and aromas of Roero Arneis, Roero Rosso, and Roero Riserva at family-run wineries such as Matteo Correggia, Malvirà, and Cascina Val del Prete. Visit vineyards overlooking the Tanaro River and the historic town of Alba to experience the beauty and bounty of Roero wine country.

Marche - Verdicchio dei Castelli di Jesi: Experience the crisp and refreshing wines of Verdicchio dei Castelli di Jesi, a DOCG wine region located in the Marche region. Taste the minerality and citrus notes of Verdicchio wines from producers such as Garofoli, Umani Ronchi, and La Staffa, and enjoy guided tastings at historic wineries and agriturismo (farm stays) in the rolling hills and mediaeval villages of the Castelli di Jesi.

Abruzzo - Pescara Valley: Discover the bold and rustic wines of the Pescara Valley, a subregion of Abruzzo known for its Montepulciano and Trebbiano grapes. Taste the rich red wines of Montepulciano d'Abruzzo and Cerasuolo d'Abruzzo, as well as crisp whites from Trebbiano d'Abruzzo, at wineries such as Masciarelli, Emidio Pepe, and Valentini. Visit vineyards nestled among the Apennine Mountains and the Adriatic Sea to experience the rugged beauty and terroir-driven wines of the Pescara Valley.

These lesser-known wine regions and experiences offer a chance to discover Italy's rich viticultural heritage and diverse terroirs, from the Alpine vineyards of Alto Adige to the volcanic slopes of Mount Etna. Whether you're tasting sparkling wines in Franciacorta, aromatic whites in Collio, or bold reds in Irpinia, these hidden gems are sure to delight wine enthusiasts and curious travellers alike.

Cooking Classes

Embarking on a cooking class in Italy is a fantastic way to immerse yourself in the country's rich culinary heritage and learn the secrets of traditional Italian cuisine. Here are some lesser-known cooking classes and culinary experiences worth exploring:

Truffle Hunting and Cooking Class in Umbria: Join a truffle hunting excursion in the forests of Umbria, accompanied by expert truffle hunters and their trained dogs. Learn how to search for these elusive fungi beneath the forest floor, and then return to a local farmhouse or agriturismo to participate in a hands-on cooking class focused on truffle-based dishes. Prepare specialties such as tagliolini al Tartufo (truffle pasta), risotto al Tartufo, and crostini with truffle-infused toppings, and savour the rich, earthy flavours of Umbrian cuisine.

Farm-to-Table Cooking Class in Tuscany: Experience the farm-to-table culinary tradition of Tuscany with a cooking class held at a local agriturismo or farmhouse in the Tuscan countryside. Harvest fresh ingredients from the garden or orchard, and then learn how to prepare traditional Tuscan dishes such as ribollita (vegetable and bread soup), pappa al pomodoro (tomato and bread soup), and peposo (Tuscan beef stew). Enjoy a leisurely meal paired with local wines, olive oil, and bread, and soak up the rustic charm and hospitality of rural Tuscany.

Seafood Cooking Class in Cinque Terre:

Discover the flavours of the Ligurian coast with a seafood cooking class held in one of the charming villages of the Cinque Terre. Visit a local fish market or harbour to select the freshest catch of the day, and then learn how to prepare classic Ligurian seafood dishes such as spaghetti alle vongole (spaghetti with clams), pesce al forno (oven-baked fish), and fritto misto di mare (mixed fried seafood). Enjoy panoramic views of the Mediterranean Sea and the colourful coastline as you cook and dine al fresco.

Pasta Making Class in Emilia-Romagna:

Explore the pasta-making traditions of Emilia-

Romagna, the culinary heartland of Italy, with a hands-on cooking class led by a local chef or pasta expert. Learn how to make fresh pasta dough from scratch using traditional techniques and locally sourced ingredients, and then master the art of shaping and cutting pasta shapes such as tagliatelle, tortellini, and ravioli. Prepare classic pasta sauces such as ragù alla bolognese (meat sauce), Pomodoro (tomato sauce), and burro e salvia (butter and sage), and enjoy a pasta feast paired with regional wines and Parmigiano Reggiano cheese.

Cheese Making Class in Piedmont:
Discover the art of cheese making in Piedmont, a region renowned for its artisanal cheeses and dairy products. Visit a local cheese farm or dairy to learn about the cheese-making process from start to finish, and then participate in a hands-on cheese-making class led by expert cheesemakers. Learn how to craft cheeses such as Toma, Robiola, and Castelmagno using traditional methods and local milk, and taste a variety of aged cheeses paired with local wines, honey, and preserves.

Pizza Making Class in Naples: Learn the secrets of authentic Neapolitan pizza with a pizza-making class held in the birthplace of pizza itself, Naples. Join a local pizzaiolo (pizza chef) in a traditional pizzeria or cooking school, and learn how to make pizza dough from scratch using simple ingredients such as flour, water, yeast, and salt. Master the art of stretching and shaping the dough, and then top your pizza with classic Neapolitan ingredients such as San Marzano tomatoes, mozzarella di bufala, and fresh basil. Bake your pizza in a wood-fired oven until it's bubbling and golden brown, and then savour the taste of true Neapolitan pizza perfection.

Gelato Making Class in Florence: Indulge your sweet tooth with a gelato-making class held in the historic city of Florence. Join a local gelato (gelato maker) in a gelateria or culinary school, and learn how to make authentic Italian gelato using fresh, seasonal ingredients and traditional techniques. Experiment with different flavours and ingredients such as pistachio, hazelnut, chocolate, and fruit, and discover the secrets to creating creamy, flavorful gelato at home. Enjoy your homemade gelato creations paired with a selection of toppings and sauces, and take-home recipes and tips for making gelato like a true Italian maestro.

These lesser-known cooking classes and culinary experiences offer a unique opportunity to learn from local experts, discover authentic Italian recipes, and immerse yourself in the rich culinary traditions of Italy. Whether you're truffle hunting in Umbria, making pasta in Emilia-Romagna, or mastering the art of Neapolitan pizza in Naples, these hidden gems are sure to leave you with a deeper appreciation for Italian food and culture.

Chapter 9

Practical Tips

Here are some practical tips to enhance your experience while exploring Italy:

Learn Some Italian Phrases: While many Italians speak English, knowing some basic Italian phrases can go a long way in making connections and navigating daily interactions.

Cash vs. Card: While credit and debit cards are widely accepted in cities and tourist areas, it's always a good idea to carry some cash, especially for smaller purchases and in more remote areas.

Public Transportation: Italy has an extensive and efficient public transportation network, including trains, buses, and metros. Consider using public transportation to get around cities and between towns, as it's often more convenient and cost-effective than driving.

Dress Appropriately: Italians tend to dress stylishly and modestly, especially when visiting religious sites or upscale restaurants. Pack clothing that is comfortable for walking and sightseeing but also appropriate for dining out.

Respect Local Customs: Italy has a rich cultural heritage, and it's important to respect local customs and traditions. Be mindful of dress codes, tipping practices, and dining etiquette, and always ask for permission before taking photos, especially in religious sites and private properties.

Stay Hydrated and Sun Protected: Italy can get hot and sunny, especially during the summer months. Stay hydrated by drinking plenty of water, and protect yourself from the sun by wearing sunscreen, a hat, and sunglasses.

Be Aware of Pickpockets: Like any tourist destination, Italy has its share of pickpockets, especially in crowded tourist areas and on public transportation. Keep your belongings secure, be vigilant in crowded places, and consider using a money belt or hidden pouch to carry valuables.

Tipping: Tipping is not as common or expected in Italy as it is in some other countries, but it's always appreciated for exceptional service. In restaurants, a service charge may be included in the bill, but you can round up or leave a small additional tip if you're satisfied with the service.

Time Management: Italians have a more relaxed approach to time, so don't be surprised if things don't always run exactly on schedule. Embrace the slower pace of life and build some flexibility into your itinerary to allow for unexpected delays or changes.

Emergency Numbers: Familiarise yourself with emergency numbers in Italy, including 112 for general emergencies, 113 for police, and 118 for medical emergencies.

By keeping these practical tips in mind, you can make the most of your time in Italy and enjoy a smooth and memorable travel experience. Buon viaggio!

Language Tips

Here are some language tips to help you navigate Italy with ease:

Basic Phrases: Learn some basic Italian phrases such as greetings (ciao - hello, Grazie - thank you), polite expressions (per favore - please, scusa - excuse me), and essential questions (dove si trova...? - where is...?).

Language Apps: Use language learning apps like Duolingo or Rosetta Stone to practise Italian before your trip. These apps offer interactive lessons and quizzes to help you improve your language skills on the go.

Phrasebook: Carry a pocket-sized phrasebook or download a language translation app on your phone for quick reference when you need to communicate with locals.

Practice Pronunciation: Italian pronunciation can be different from English, so practise speaking aloud to improve your pronunciation and accent.

Language Exchange: Consider participating in a language exchange program where you can practise Italian with native speakers in exchange for helping them learn your language.

Watch Italian Movies or TV Shows: Watching Italian movies or TV shows with subtitles can help you get accustomed to the language, improve your listening skills, and pick up on common phrases and expressions.

Take a Language Course: If you have the time and resources, enrol in a language course either online or in-person to gain a more comprehensive understanding of Italian grammar, vocabulary, and conversational skills.

Immerse Yourself: Immerse yourself in the language and culture by engaging with locals, ordering food in Italian, and trying to have conversations in Italian whenever possible.

Be Patient and Persistent: Learning a new language takes time and practice, so be patient with yourself and keep practising regularly to improve your skills over time.

Have Fun: Learning a new language can be a rewarding and enjoyable experience, so have fun with it! Embrace the opportunity to immerse yourself in Italian culture and connect with people from all walks of life.

Transportation

Navigating transportation in Italy is relatively easy thanks to its well-developed network of trains, buses, and metros. Here are some tips to help you get around:

Trains: Italy's train system, operated by Trenitalia and Italo, connects major cities and towns across the country. High-speed trains like Frecciarossa and Frecciargento are efficient for long-distance travel, while regional trains are great for shorter journeys and exploring smaller towns. Purchase tickets in advance for the best prices, and be sure to validate them before boarding regional trains.

Buses: Local and regional buses are a convenient way to reach destinations not served by trains, especially in rural areas. Companies like FlixBus and MarinoBus offer affordable intercity bus services between major cities, while local buses provide transportation within cities and towns. Tickets can usually be purchased onboard or at ticket kiosks.

Metro: Italy has metro systems in major cities like Rome, Milan, Naples, Turin, and Palermo, offering quick and efficient transportation within urban areas. Purchase tickets at metro stations or tobacco shops, and validate them before entering the metro platform.

Taxis: Taxis are readily available in most Italian cities and can be hailed on the street or booked in advance. Be sure to use licensed taxis with metres, and always ask for a fare estimate before starting your journey. Uber is available in some cities, including Milan and Rome.

Car Rentals: Renting a car can be convenient for exploring rural areas and regions with limited public transportation. Major car rental companies operate at airports and in city centres but be aware of traffic congestion, limited parking, and restricted driving zones in historic city centres.

Biking: Many Italian cities offer bike-sharing programs and dedicated bike lanes, making cycling a convenient and eco-friendly option for getting around. Rent a bike from a bike-sharing station or a local rental shop, and explore cities like Florence, Bologna, and Lucca on two wheels.

Walking: Italy's compact city centres and pedestrian-friendly streets make walking a pleasant and practical way to explore. Wear comfortable shoes use a map or GPS to navigate, and take advantage of guided walking tours to discover hidden gems and historical landmarks.

Boats and Ferries: In coastal regions and islands like Venice, Capri, and the Amalfi Coast, boats and ferries provide scenic transportation between towns and attractions. Purchase tickets at ticket offices or online, and enjoy stunning views of the coastline and the Mediterranean Sea.

By familiarising yourself with Italy's transportation options and planning your journeys, you can make the most of your time in this beautiful country and explore its diverse landscapes, historic cities, and charming towns with ease.

Safety Tips

When travelling in Italy, it's essential to prioritise your safety. Here are some safety tips to keep in mind during your visit:

Stay Aware of Your Surroundings: Be mindful of your surroundings, especially in crowded tourist areas, public transportation, and busy city streets. Stay alert and aware of your belongings to prevent theft or pickpocketing.

Use Secure Accommodations: Choose reputable hotels, hostels, or vacation rentals with good reviews and secure facilities. Lock your room and valuables when you're not present, and use hotel safes for passports, cash, and other valuables.

Stay Connected: Keep important phone numbers handy, including emergency contacts, local police, and your country's embassy or consulate. Make sure your phone is charged and has access to local emergency services.

Travel Insurance: Consider purchasing travel insurance to cover medical emergencies, trip cancellations, and other unforeseen events. Verify that your policy includes coverage for activities you plan to engage in, such as hiking, skiing, or water sports.

Avoid Solo Travel at Night: Avoid walking alone at night, especially in unfamiliar or poorly lit areas. Use reputable transportation options such as taxis or rideshare services, and stick to well-lit, populated streets when walking after dark.

Be Cautious with Strangers: Exercise caution when interacting with strangers, especially if they seem overly friendly or insistent. Politely decline offers of assistance or unsolicited services, and trust your instincts if something feels off.

Respect Local Laws and Customs: Familiarise yourself with local laws, customs, and cultural norms, and adhere to them during your visit. Respect religious sites, dress codes, and local traditions, and be mindful of behaviour that may be considered disrespectful or offensive.

Emergency Preparedness: Be prepared for emergencies by carrying essential items such as a first aid kit, medications, and a photocopy of your passport and travel documents. Familiarise yourself with emergency procedures at your accommodation and know how to access medical care if needed.

Stay Hydrated and Sun Safe: Italy can experience high temperatures, especially during the summer months. Stay hydrated by drinking plenty of water, wear sunscreen, a hat, and sunglasses to protect yourself from the sun, and seek shade during the hottest parts of the day.

Trust Your Instincts: Trust your instincts and intuition if you feel uncomfortable or unsafe in a situation. If you sense danger or need assistance, don't hesitate to seek help from local authorities or trusted individuals.

By staying vigilant, informed, and prepared, you can enjoy a safe and memorable experience while exploring Italy's rich culture, history, and natural beauty.

Conclusion

As your journey through Italy comes to an end, reflect on the unforgettable experiences, flavours, and sights you've encountered along the way. From the bustling streets of Rome to the tranquil hills of Tuscany, Italy has captured your heart with its rich history, vibrant culture, and warm hospitality.

As you bid farewell to this enchanting country, carry with you the memories of ancient ruins, Renaissance art, and delicious culinary delights. Whether you've explored hidden gems off the beaten path or indulged in the iconic landmarks of Italy's most famous cities, your time in Italy has been nothing short of extraordinary.

As you return home, may the beauty and charm of Italy stay with you, inspiring you to embrace adventure, savour life's pleasures, and cherish the moments that make travel truly transformative. Grazie mille, Italia, for an unforgettable journey. Until we meet again, arrivederci!

Resources

Here are some resources to help you further explore Italy and plan your next adventure:

Tourism Websites: Visit the official tourism websites for Italy and its regions to access information on attractions, accommodations, transportation, and events:

Italy Tourism: www.italia.it

Visit Tuscany: www.visittuscany.com

Visit Sicily: www.visitsicily.info

Visit Lombardy: www.in-lombardia.com

Travel Guides: Invest in travel guides such as Lonely Planet, Rick Steves, or DK Eyewitness Travel for comprehensive information, insider tips, and suggested itineraries.

Online Forums: Join online travel forums like TripAdvisor, Lonely Planet's Thorn Tree, or Rick Steves' Travel Forum to connect with fellow travellers, ask questions, and share advice and recommendations.

Language Learning Apps: Use language learning apps like Duolingo, Babbel, or Rosetta Stone to improve your Italian language skills and enhance your travel experience.

Cooking Classes: Search for cooking classes and culinary experiences in Italy on websites like Airbnb Experiences, Cookly, or Viator to learn how to cook authentic Italian dishes from local chefs and experts.

Transportation Services: Access transportation services and book tickets for trains, buses, and ferries through official websites such as Trenitalia, Italo, and FlixBus.

Accommodation Booking: Use online booking platforms like Booking.com, Airbnb, or Hotels.com to find and reserve accommodations that suit your preferences and budget.

Cultural Events: Check local event listings, cultural calendars, and social media pages for information on festivals, exhibitions, concerts, and other cultural events happening during your visit.

Travel Insurance: Purchase travel insurance from reputable providers like World Nomads, Allianz Travel, or AXA Assistance to protect yourself against unexpected emergencies and travel disruptions.

Local Recommendations: Seek recommendations and insider tips from locals, hotel staff, and tour guides to discover hidden gems, authentic experiences, and lesser-known attractions in Italy.

With these resources at your fingertips, you'll be well-equipped to continue your exploration of Italy and create unforgettable memories on your next journey. Buon viaggio!

Useful Websites

Here are some useful websites to assist you in planning your trip to Italy:

Italy Tourism Official Website: The official tourism website for Italy provides comprehensive information on destinations, attractions, accommodations, transportation, and more: [Italy Tourism](https://www.italia.it/en/home.html)

Lonely Planet Italy: Lonely Planet offers travel guides, tips, and advice for exploring Italy's cities, regions, and countryside: [Lonely Planet Italy](https://www.lonelyplanet.com/italy)

TripAdvisor: TripAdvisor features reviews, ratings, and recommendations from travellers on accommodations, restaurants, attractions, and activities in Italy: [TripAdvisor Italy](https://www.tripadvisor.com/Tourism-g187768-Italy-Vacations.html)

Booking.com: Booking.com allows you to search and book accommodations, including hotels, apartments, villas, and hostels, in cities and towns across Italy: [Booking.com Italy](https://www.booking.com/country/it.en.html)

Trenitalia: Trenitalia is Italy's national railway company, offering train schedules, ticket bookings, and travel information for train travel within Italy: [Trenitalia](https://www.trenitalia.com/en.html)

Italo: Italo is a high-speed train operator in Italy, providing modern and comfortable train services between major cities: [Italo](https://www.italotreno.it/en)

Rome2rio: Rome2rio is a comprehensive travel search engine that helps you plan your journey by providing information on transportation options, routes, and travel times between destinations in Italy: [Rome2rio](https://www.rome2rio.com/)

Italy Magazine: Italy Magazine offers articles, guides, and insights into Italian culture, cuisine, history, and lifestyle: [Italy Magazine](https://www.italymagazine.com/)

Eating Italy Food Tours: Eating Italy Food Tours offers guided culinary tours and experiences in cities like Rome, Florence, and Venice, allowing you to discover Italy's gastronomic delights: [Eating Italy Food Tours](https://www.eatingeurope.com/)

Italy With Kids: Italy With Kids provides family-friendly travel tips, activities, and recommendations for exploring Italy with children: [Italy With Kids](https://www.italywithkids.com/)

These websites offer valuable resources and information to help you plan and make the most of your trip to Italy. Whether you're looking for accommodation, transportation, sightseeing tips, or culinary experiences, these websites have you covered.

Recommended Reading

Here are some recommended reading materials to further immerse yourself in Italian culture, history, and literature:

"Italy: A History" by Vincent Cronin: This comprehensive history of Italy provides a detailed overview of the country's rich and diverse past, from ancient civilizations to the present day.

"Under the Tuscan Sun" by Frances Mayes: Follow the author's journey of restoring an abandoned villa in Tuscany and discovering the beauty, charm, and culinary delights of rural Italy.

"Inferno" by Dan Brown: Join symbologist Robert Langdon as he unravels a mystery set against the backdrop of Florence, Venice, and Istanbul, exploring famous landmarks and uncovering hidden secrets.

"My Brilliant Friend" by Elena Ferrante: Dive into the captivating Neapolitan Novels series, which follows the lifelong friendship of two women against the backdrop of postwar Naples.

"The Leopard" by Giuseppe Tomasi di Lampedusa: Set in 19th-century Sicily, this classic novel explores the decline of the Sicilian aristocracy and the social and political changes sweeping across Italy.

"The Agony and the Ecstasy" by Irving Stone: Delve into the life of Renaissance artist Michelangelo Buonarroti in this biographical novel, which vividly portrays his struggles, triumphs, and artistic genius.

"A Farewell to Arms" by Ernest Hemingway: Experience the romance and tragedy of World War I through the eyes of American ambulance driver Frederic Henry in this classic novel set in Italy.

"The Birth of Venus" by Sarah Dunant: Transport yourself to Renaissance Florence and follow the journey of a young woman who becomes entangled in art, passion, and political intrigue.

"Italian Folktales" by Italo Calvino: Discover a collection of enchanting and timeless folktales from across Italy, retold by one of Italy's greatest writers.

"Brunelleschi's Dome: How a Renaissance Genius Reinvented Architecture" by Ross King: Explore the fascinating story behind the construction of Florence's iconic dome, a masterpiece of Renaissance engineering and innovation.

These books offer insights into Italy's history, culture, art, and literature, allowing you to deepen your understanding and appreciation of this captivating country. Whether you're interested in historical fiction, travel memoirs, or classic literature, there's something for every reader to enjoy.

Maps and Apps

Here are some maps and apps that will be useful during your travels in Italy:

Google Maps: Google Maps offers detailed maps, directions, and navigation for exploring cities, towns, and countryside in Italy. You can also use it to find nearby attractions, restaurants, and public transportation options.

Citymapper: Citymapper provides real-time transit information, including bus, metro, tram, and bike-sharing options, in major cities like Rome, Milan, and Florence. It also offers step-by-step navigation and estimated travel times.

Rome2rio: Rome2rio is a comprehensive travel planning app that helps you find the best transportation options between cities and towns in Italy, including trains, buses, flights, and ferries.

Moovit: Moovit offers public transit information and real-time arrival times for buses, trams, and metros in cities across Italy. It also provides service alerts and trip-planning tools to help you navigate public transportation networks.

Trenitalia: The Trenitalia app allows you to search train schedules, book tickets, and access your reservations for train travel within Italy. You can also use it to check real-time train status and platform information.

Italo: Italo is the official app for Italo high-speed trains, offering ticket bookings, schedules, and travel information for journeys between major cities in Italy.

Maps.me: Maps. I provide detailed offline maps for Italy, allowing you to navigate without an internet connection. You can download maps of specific regions or cities in advance and use them to find your way around with GPS navigation.

WhatsApp: WhatsApp is a popular messaging app that allows you to stay connected with friends, family, and fellow travellers while in Italy. You can use it to send messages, make voice calls, and share photos and videos over Wi-Fi or mobile data.

XE Currency Converter: XE Currency Converter provides real-time exchange rates and currency conversion for over 180 currencies, including the Euro (EUR) used in Italy. It's useful for calculating prices and expenses in your home currency.

Italian Phrasebook: Download a language translation app or Italian phrasebook to help you communicate with locals and navigate daily interactions in Italian. Apps like Duolingo, Babbel, or Rosetta Stone can also help you improve your language skills before and during your trip.

With these maps and apps at your fingertips, you'll be well-equipped to navigate Italy's cities, countryside, and transportation networks with ease and confidence.

Printed in Great Britain
by Amazon